Stand Up!

A journey of finding strength leads to a unique model of
practice in exploring relationships with Self, Horse, and Others.

PAMELA N. JEFFERS

authorHOUSE

AuthorHouse™
1663 Liberty Drive
Bloomington, IN 47403
www.authorhouse.com
Phone: 1 (800) 839-8640

Published by AuthorHouse   03/24/2017

ISBN: 978-1-5246-8415-0 (sc)
ISBN: 978-1-5246-8413-6 (hc)
ISBN: 978-1-5246-8414-3 (e)

Library of Congress Control Number: 2017904138

Print information available on the last page.

Contents

Acknowledgements

I wish to thank my family and friends for all their support, patience and encouragement not only while writing the book but more importantly throughout my life's' journey. Mom and Dad, even though you did not understand my love for horses at such an early age, you supported it and I am deeply appreciative of the love and willingness to commit financially and emotionally to this undying love I had for them, then and now. Your support set the stage for future endeavors. My first horse, Penny, meant so much to me. She was a gift beyond belief and I am deeply grateful that your love for me allowed me to grow, learn and love her as a youth. It was the catalyst of my life long pursuit of learning through horses.

This entire journey that led to this book would not have been possible without the love and support of my wonderful husband and children. Robert, you are a kind, loving, hardworking man who has stood by me no matter what. You gave me encouragement and support to "find my voice" and write the book. You have always supported my love of horses and I deeply appreciate your endless love for me. I admire and appreciate your wisdom and strength and I am so thankful to have you as my life long partner to navigate this journey together. LaTicia and Cameron, you are my pride and joy. You gave me the strength and inspiration to STAND UP! It is with great pride in my heart to bear witness to your own life journey as you bring your gifts to the world.

I would like to acknowledge my siblings patience and love as well as friends who have been there for our family.

A very special thank you to the herd of horses that led our family down this beautiful path and continue to support us each and every day: K.C., Coco, Pepper, Cheyenne, Angel, Snick, Scoot, Amicka, Tango, Cookie, Fiona, Nikki and William. Additionally, thank you Kia, Rowdy, Kitty and Smokie for walking along with us on this journey.

I wish to extend a big thank you to all the brave professionals and agencies that took a chance on partnering with us. Natural Freedom would not be in existence without you and I wish to thank all the mental health providers who graciously shared the knowledge, support and expertise. Also, I am thankful for all the pioneers in both fields, equine and behavioral health, that have completed research, written about findings, experiences and knowledge. I would also like to thank the professionals that have guided us in clinical supervision along the way.

Both LaTica and Mom have an amazing creative eye and I appreciate your willingness to share your beautiful photographs for the book. Also, I am thankful to LaTicia for sharing this creative gift to create the cover design and photograph as well and Lisa for agreeing to edit the book. Your time, effort and expertise are greatly appreciated.

A big thank you goes out to Janessa Bartlett for joining our Natural Freedom team. You are a kind-hearted, loving, compassionate person whom is a wonderful asset and gift to our services and team. Your motivation and willingness to assist as needed to complete the book was deeply appreciated. I am so thankful and proud to have you on our team and as our extended family.

Lastly, thank you to all the individuals, groups and families that have trusted us to provide services. It is a blessing to be a part of your journey.

Disclaimer

I have studied horsemanship for the past 40+ years through reading magazine articles, books, attending demonstrations, clinics and trainings. I attempted to give credit to the best of my ability; however I cannot recollect exactly the originality of all the knowledge received over the years. Additionally, the journey of studying spirituality holds the same truth. For all those pioneers of knowledge thank you for sharing your wisdom.

Chapter 1
Family Time

Slam...Slam.... All four horses loaded and ready to go!
Sundays were set aside for family activities. Sometimes

the Sunday activity consisted of practicing shooting our longbows, sometimes it was trail-riding on the family farm, and sometimes it was combining the two activities with mounted archery. But regardless of the activity, I tried very hard to set aside Sundays for family time together.

My husband, Robert, was a very hard-working man, a fourth-generation dairy farmer who worked ten-hour days, six or seven days a week. He had every other Sunday off. The Sundays that he was scheduled to milk the cows we enjoyed our family time close to home. However, we were all excited that today was his day off! This gave us the opportunity to load up and take the horses to Robert's sister's place, 45 minutes south towards to Ohio River.

As we made our way through the brushy, scarcely used trail, I was keeping a watchful eye on the family and their mounts as I navigated riding the green horse. It was Cheyenne's first trail ride away from home. Things were going along relatively smoothly until the unexpected happened....Robert's horse, Coco, stepped directly on a hornets' nest! Coco tried with all her might to take care of him. Robert had little time to perfect his horsemanship skills at this time in his busy life, but he had the strength of an ox and was riding a mare that was all heart! With hornets swirling all around her, she cantered in place until he managed to grab hold of a tree. With a strong hold on the tree, he smacked her on the rump to give her permission to run so she could find relief from the situation. Meanwhile, as the hornets were swirling in the

2

air, they made their way to our son's pony. Cameron and his pony, Pepper, happened to be in a small stream bed, and when I looked up to find them I watched as she slowly knelt down into the water. I yelled to him, "Jump off—she is going down!" He escaped safely and stood in the water beside his pony. Our daughter LaTicia had been leading the four of us riding our solid, foundation Quarter Horse trail mount KC, and I was bringing up the rear, so we managed to escape the swirl of very angry hornets.

Coco ran ten or fifteen feet before turning to find us. Robert and I quickly went into action to assess the damage of the situation. Immediately, we found that Cameron had been stung multiple times. Several years back, Cameron had had what the medical field called an "atypical" reaction to multiple bee stings while being with us as we put hay in the hay mound. At that time, we were told that the traditional treatment of an Epi pen was not helpful to him, and that if he were to get stung again we should get him to an emergency room as soon as possible. As we all quickly remounted to scurry back through the unmarked trails, my head was swirling. The local hospital had just closed and we were deep in the hills of southeast Ohio in rural, underserved Meigs County. I knew we had to act fast and make some tough decisions.

We finally reached the clearing and could see our horse trailer. As we made our way to the trailer I had my right foot already out of the stirrup and halfway swung over my horse, Cheyenne. As my feet hit the ground, I swiftly untacked the girth holding the saddle and swung the saddle to the ground. Next, I took off the bridle. At this point, I was guessing I would find him with the other horses running through Meigs County later. But in the moment I had bigger priorities. Robert had done the same with Coco, and LaTicia followed suit. All four horses were grazing on the grass as we scooped up our nine year old and ran him into Robert's sister's house. Luckily, she had some options available to us. We drew a bath, applied the typical solutions, and waited.

An hour or so later, the waiting was over and we were in the clear. Cameron was far from comfortable, but he was not in a life-threatening situation. But, as we took our sigh of relief we both realized the day was far from over. Who knew where the horses were by now?! As we prepared for what we thought may be a "search and rescue mission" for four lost horses in the middle of nowhere, much to our relief and surprise, we opened the door to find them all standing within fifteen feet of the trailer. They were standing there as calm and relaxed as if they were at home. We opened the doors to the trailer, and one by one each came to us. We slipped their halters on as we loaded each one into the trailer to go home.

Slam…Slam….as the doors closed, Robert and I glanced at each other with pride in our eyes and smiles on our faces—what a great herd of horses we have! Little did I know, at the time, how true that statement would prove to be.

Chapter 2
Dreaming?

Knock...Knock... the sound came from the front door on this cool September morning in 2002. We had received the strangest phone call several weeks earlier: "Mr. Jeffers, there are funds available to improve land along the creek that runs through the Jeffers Property. We would like to discuss our thoughts and plans on how this could improve your farm and assist it in moving into the future." Interested and excited at the possible stroke of luck, we scheduled the meeting.

Representatives from two different governmental agencies began the conversation by explaining that there had been a hazardous-material spill from the Meigs County Coal Mine #31 in 1993. A lawsuit resulted in the Southern Ohio Coal Company (SOCCO) and American Electric Power (AEP) paying fines. Before they paid the fines, however, they attempted to use old farming practices as their defense in the lawsuit. In 1993, Jeffers Farm consisted of 1200+ acres and was situated in the same watershed as the spillage. Over the years, the money from the settlement had sat idle, collected interest and now totaled $3.2 million dollars. We were informed that the fine money was to be used to improve land practices along the effected watershed, and since we were listed in the legal report they were interested in starting by providing assistance to the Jeffers Family Farm.

What appeared to be a stroke of luck quickly turned into our biggest nightmare. It was filled with twists and turns of anguish, anger, frustration and, ultimately, the realization of our deepest fears.

Trying to navigate the endless specifications and countless inspections of multiple agencies, all with different expectations and interpretations of requirements, led us down a twisted, chaotic journey; emotionally, physically and financially. All of our thoughts, energy, time and money soon got sucked into what we called "The Barn Project." With little or no time left to attend to our small businesses, which we had worked to piece together in order to supplement a weak income-base of dairy-farming, our world as we knew it gradually crumbled and burned, like a log that slowly turns into ashes. Our hope of a brighter tomorrow withered slowly away. Once it was gone, everything revolved around the basics of daily living. One by one, our rental properties were sold off to pay mortgages, medical expenses and just plain daily expenses. Four years from the time the government agency representatives knocked on our door, we had cashed in everything we had: retirement funds, mutual funds, and savings all gone! And then the creditors' calls began.... dreaming? NO! This was a nightmare! A nightmare that took four and half years of agencies on the premises; the residual effects lasted another six years.

Robert in the milking parlor in the new dairy facility.

Chapter 3
The Ride

Ring….Ring…. It was early evening when the phone rang. It must have been around 6:00, and I remember thinking, he must need help with his math homework again. Cameron's best friend called him around this time when he needed some help with his homework. As I picked up the phone my heart sank, my knees got weak. What? No!! It was a fellow soccer Mom calling to give us the horrible news... his friend had died in a hunting accident earlier in the day. We were speechless, stunned and in utter disbelief.

It was November 2005, and for the past three years we had been jumping through the hoops of the now-mandated governmental barn project. Things had been moving along well until earlier this year. In reflection, the call informing us of his friend's fatal accident seemed to be the pivotal point of the rapid spiral out of control. The year 2006 became the year of chaos, pain, fear and agony that each of our family members experienced in different ways. As a mother, watching it spiral was like having one foot in the stirrup while getting dragged over cobble stones, dirt and thorns.

"It is upon disaster that good fortune rests." This quote by a Taoist sage, Lao-tzu, kept resurfacing over and over in my head. At first it came with a laugh and a sarcastic, snide thought and comment. As my family plummeted down, spiraling out of control, the idea of good fortune was becoming a thought beyond recognition. And I watched in confusion and disbelief as my family members began to take on wholly new personae.

Cameron shut everyone out, all his friends and us too. He started hanging out with what the teachers referred to during a parent/teacher conference as "not Cameron's crowd." Cameron was a straight-A student until this year, when his grades dropped to Ds and even an F. He was angry and bitter at the world, and it took great effort to get him to school. Sometimes he just refused to go. Meanwhile, LaTicia was experiencing peer relationship issues that can be all too common during the high school years. She was randomly fainting and the doctors could not find out why. They suggested a special diet and more medical tests. We maxed out one of the credit cards paying for this test and that test, but still there were no answers. At this point Robert was giving up too. There were times when I literally had to take his hand and force him to shower. The strong hard-working man I married was being whittled away before my eyes! At one point I wrote in my journal:

> *I feel like I am in a batting cage, trapped with no way out, fast balls, curve balls all sailing past me and my family members at 98 mph. I started the batting practice with some good solid swings but as the machine picked up the pace I soon began ducking and dodging until I felt like curling up in a fetal position just taking the hits hoping and praying the machine would short-circuit and stop or at very least run out of balls! As I lie in the fetal position, crying and gasping for a breath I would hold on to the Lao-tzu's words and hoping it was not just words on a piece of paper.*

There were days I felt like staying in bed and curling up as in my journal entry. However, some days were better than others so we pushed on. And in losing ourselves we slowly, steadily and eventually all found ourselves each with our own pace, hurdles and triumphs but all with the help of a family of horses. They helped us, as we remembered how to live again!

Chapter 4

Hurting Together Leads
to Herding Together

In the midst of the chaos the four of us had splintered, gone our separate ways. Long gone were the days of Sunday family-fun trail rides, archery practices and hiking. We barely managed to put food on the table, and the energy to enjoy life had slowly and progressively moved into energy to keep creditors at bay, juggling the bills to keep ahead of the imminent doom of collapse. As we navigated the chaos, many of the decisions we made, might appear to the naked eye to be very counter-intuitive. Maybe it was the years of horse-handling, or the fact that I was tired of jumping through everybody else's hoops, but the" Momma Bear" gradually began to emerge. Even though we received many snide comments and projected judgements against many of our decisions, I knew we had to come together to heal. Come together, just like our herd of horses, we needed to put back the pieces and feel the *connection* within the family that had slowly disintegrated over the past four years.

Our place sits on top of a large hill, and as a result we receive high winds. On one occasion, many years later, we experienced straight-line winds that reached upwards of 80 mph. We had just turned the herd out, and they grazed happily until the winds picked up speed. They weren't far from the house, so I was able to observe them as the storm moved into the area. As the winds picked up, the horses came galloping back towards the barn from the first hill out. Instead of running in the usual line formation, however, they were formed in a very tight nucleus, running with hair touching hair of each horse. They ran in unison in a full gallop, making turns together, as a unit, similar to a school of fish or a flock of birds. As they made it to the flat area directly behind the barn, at a full gallop, they made a circle to the right, circling around together in unison, not missing a step, all together not as individuals but as a unit!

In that moment, in the midst of the chaos of the winds swirling around and as our metal roof was floating through the air like a crumpled piece of paper, I realized that this was what my intuition had told me years earlier. In 2006, I had absolutely no logical reason why it would be a good idea to bring the children back home to bear witness on a daily basis to our new reality. And at the time, I questioned myself regularly, "Is this a good idea? Do the children really need to see the pain their parents are enduring from the chaos?" But intuitively I just knew that to heal we needed to come together and I needed to bring the family together. We were all enduring individual pains within ourselves and trying to navigate them individually, without a sense of **connection**. So against popular opinion, I resisted the overwhelming urge to follow my logical brain and I brought the family together. Once again, life's lessons came from our trusted herd of horses. Just like the horses, we came together in the scariest moment to remember what a family unit feels like, looks like and acts like.

It was one of the hardest and easiest decisions all rolled into one....in the fall of 2006 both children came home for homeschool instruction, and we began herding together through the hurt.

Chapter 5

Sorting Through the Chaos

Having spent my whole life with horses, I knew as a horse-handler that you need to have a clear idea of expectations in the horse/human relationship, or the horse will create it for you. For example, if you have poor boundaries and lack in acknowledgement and/or action to establish appropriate boundaries, before long the horse will be a pushy and difficult to handle. Ray Hunt is quoted as saying, "Don't try to go through something bad and come out good...stop and start over." And I guess that is what I wanted for the family. We were pushing through a tough time, going separate ways, and I wanted it to just STOP! It needed to stop, we needed to start over. The year 2006 ended up being a strange year of fact-finding to help our logical brain make sense of the chaos, mixed with learning holistic methods to aid in healing, and topped off with gaining strength and believing in hope.

Together, as we settled into our new reality, we were no longer running in circles, jumping through the hoops of perceivable expectations. To the naked eye we were giving up, and admittedly there were days when we did. For the most part, however, we juggled taking care of the barn full of horses that was our traditional business. Our days were filled with taking care of the horses in for boarding, training and giving lessons, homeschooling, and reading books on healing.

Between these duties, I attempted to try to figure out the meaning behind the copy of a letter that one of the government employees had handed to us months earlier. Apparently, he was just as frustrated and confused about the direction of the project. The contents could be the answer to WHY? As things spiraled out of control, Robert and I constantly had the question burning in our thoughts: Why? Why are so many "big wigs" from local, state and federal governments inundating a simple family living in the middle of nowhere? Why?

In my spare time, I started to take on the look of Erin Brockovich, diving into all the farming statistics, and desperately attempting to understand all the governmental agencies involved in our once-simple farm family: the United States Dept. of Agriculture (USDA), United States Fish and Wildlife Service (USFWS), Natural Resource Conservation Service (NRCS), Ohio

Department of Natural Resources (ODNR), Soil and Water Conservation Department (SWCD), Department of Interior (DOI), Natural Resource Damage Assessment (NRDA), Environmental Protection Agency (EPA), EQIP Funds, Leading Creek Improvement Funds, Cherry Report and Environmental Covenant. All of these agencies, programs and/or funds were involved in our lives for the previous four years. We had met with their representatives, had inspections through them, signed funding agreements with them, or been threatened by them. Sometimes they came together in a unifying team approach, sometimes alone. But intuitively I felt there had to be a bigger reason why so many governmental powerhouse agencies would take up so much of their interest, time, energy and money for a farm family that had not asked for any of their programs, funds or services, and regretted ever meeting with them that cool September morning in 2002.

But we had, and now I had a burning desire to understand what we had really gotten ourselves into. My whole life has revolved around horses, and I draw on so many life lessons and personal growth opportunities from the time spent with them. Thus, my brain just kept going back to another Ray Hunt saying, "It's what happened before what happened." So, what happened? What was truly going on, and how did the dream turn to the nightmare? How did the intent of the meetings go from "we are here to help" to the threats, manipulations of specifications, guidelines and arguments between us and them, them and contract workers, them against themselves? The letter dated August 17, 2005 was where I could start.

Chapter 6

Library Visit

In the midst of my diving into researching the meaning of the letter, more medical issues presented themselves, so the letter had to wait. By early spring, the stress had started to grab hold of Robert physically. He was experiencing lower-back issues, difficulty sleeping and functioning, and even black-out spells. By the fall of 2006, Robert's blood pressure was so high that the doctor wanted to hospitalize him. None of the treatments was working. I was desperate! We could not afford a hospital bill any more than we could afford to lose Robert! So, in a desperate act of love through the lens of fear, I made a trip to the local library. I had to have looked like a hoarder of books leaving with two huge bags of self-help books, tapes and DVDs on holistic healing methods.

My family thought I had lost my mind as they watched me scour the books all spread out on the living room floor! "Here, let's try this; How about this? Now, let's do this," they would hear me say on a daily basis…. Aromatherapy, yoga, herbs, diet, exercise, the list went on. Where do we begin?

Everyone was reluctant to join me at first, but I had to do something! I had to stop the swirling thoughts in my own head: How could this have happened? Was it a cover-up for something bigger than us? Was it a power struggle between agencies? Was it our fear turned to anger that led us down this path?" STOP…STOP…STOP….please STOP the madness of my own thoughts! But how? I was so desperate to "Stop and Start Over" like the Ray Hunt saying that I slowly grabbed the yoga VHS tape that was at the bottom of the bag filled with library books. "Have I lost my mind?" I asked myself. The cover photo was of a lady wearing a turban. "Oh, why not give it try?" I told myself. "I have to get out of the batter's cage that I described in my journal somehow!"

"Kundalini Yoga for Balanced Chakras with Guutej" was the name of the tape. At first I struggled to get through it, and the entire family laughed at me and the "Turban Lady," but I stayed with it and slowly started to practice the breathing styles used in the program. And when I added the lavender essential oil it seemed to give my swirling thoughts some relief.

One day Robert was experiencing a particularly difficult day. He no longer had the strength to fight off my ridiculous library-book-fueled ideas, and he accepted my encouragement to go for a walk. "But I don't want to go for a walk," he said at first. "We won't go far, I promise," I told him. As we made our way to the flat past the barn he stated, "That's it, that's far enough." I asked him to sit cross-legged on the ground, and he did. I got behind him and gently massaged his temples, instructing him to breathe in and out, in line with the methods I had been practicing with the "Turban Lady."

We were sitting on a blanket in a horse pasture of 70-plus acres. The horses were within sight, but not close to us. Within minutes of our breathing exercise, however, one of the paint horses, Cheyenne, slowly strolled over to us. I fought off the thought of getting up, as it was the first time I had been able to engage Robert in any of the "holistic" techniques I had researched. We were both so beaten-down and exhausted that the traditional safety-measures of the horse world were the least of our worries or concerns.

As we sat there in the middle of that pasture, the most amazing thing occurred, of a sort I had never allowed myself to experience with the horses before. I had always gone to the barn with an agenda in my head for a training-session with a horse, or had the lesson goal for a riding-lesson, grooming, and so forth. But today was different, and I, we, were finally ready to *slow down* and receive it. Slowly and gently, Cheyenne positioned himself directly in front of Robert. He softly placed his muzzle on the crown of his head. It did not matter how high or low Robert's head moved—Cheyenne would keep his muzzle with him.

Eventually, the other horses became curious and worked their way closer to us. Cheyenne had other plans, though, and refused to let them come close to us! If any of the other herd members got closer than fifteen feet, Cheyenne would pin his ears and run them off. He would then return to the exact same spot, resuming his position over Robert, *breathing in and out* in unison. Forty-five minutes later, Cheyenne lifted his head, casually re-joined the herd and "returned to grazing." Robert slowly lifted his head and with tears in his eyes stated, "I feel better than I have in a long time....It feels like 1000 pounds have been lifted from my shoulders."

It was time! It was time to "pull ourselves up by the boot straps." It was time to uncurl ourselves from the fetal position in that "batter's cage," and look the machine square in the eyes! Oh, thoughts of the injustice and victimization of "The Barn Project" still creep into our minds. And those "could have, should have, have to" thoughts manage to sneak in when I least expect them, but with the *power of the breath* I learned from the "Turban Lady" and now practice daily with the herd of horses, I have learned that I am in control of those thoughts! I was in control of the metaphoric machine of spiraling thoughts the whole time. The whole time, I had the power to turn off the machine and STAND UP! Thankfully, Cheyenne knew we needed the lesson, and thankfully, we were ready to receive it!

Chapter 7
The Climb

The journey to STAND UP and look the metaphorical pitching machine in the eye was not a smooth one; no, it took many twists and turns along the way. Many times, it had the look and feel of a rock climber scaling what seemed an impossible height. As our family teetered with toes barely-secured to the surface of the mountain, we would reach for a ledge here or a crevice there. Desperately, we searched for the next lip of a rock in the mountain surface to pull ourselves up as we slowly pulled ourselves up and worked our way back into living. And the journey from surviving to thriving began.

The trips to the library had not stopped. We immersed ourselves in many more books. The books I read varied, ranging from Eat, Pray, Love by Elizabeth Gilbert to books by Deepak Chopra, Eckert Tolle and many others. But each in its own unique way gave me a lending-hand to the climb out of the "batter's cage." While Robert studied various religious and cultural beliefs by reading books such as Ancient Wisdom, Modern World: Ethics for a New Millennium by the Dalai Lama and Awakening the Buddha Within by Lama Surya Das, I gradually found books about horses and spirituality. The Tao of Equus by Linda Kohanov was the book that put all the pieces of my life together! It all made sense! I had had no idea that equine-facilitated learning even existed, but I was overjoyed to have found the book.

Years earlier, as a young seventeen-year-old, I had been involved in a therapeutic riding program called "Hope on Horseback." My 4-H advisor had started a small, modest program with a few members of our 4-H group. I took great pride in preparing my Standardbred/Quarter Horse Cross mare, Penny, for the crutches and wheelchairs that she would need to be comfortable with to play a part in the program. It had such an impact on me that I chose therapeutic recreation as my major in college, and my master's thesis concept was "The Effects of Horseback Riding on Individuals with Cerebral Palsy." Upon graduation, however, I quickly discovered that starting a therapeutic riding program was very costly, and that it would be difficult to make a living in this way. So over the years, the initial dream of providing a therapeutic horse program had gradually faded away as the new goal of raising two beautiful children had surfaced.

After reading Linda's book, however, I was intrigued. Could I perhaps rekindle this old passion that had been put on the shelf? Could this provide the extra income we so desperately needed right now?

Robert and I knew we had to have a plan. The "dream come true" had led the family dairy farm into a place where it appeared as though it would not sustain the three families it had prior to that meeting in September of 2002. We had sold our six rental properties, and the supplemental income was long gone. So, as we slowly started to STAND UP to the pitching machine, we knew we had to do something to increase our income. We had already explored a number of options. Robert was too old to join the service and he missed the age cut-off for CXS railroad work by months. I looked for jobs in my professional field back in my hometown. But we truly did not want to leave our farm, and we were eager to explore all the options to make something work. My traditional small part-time horse business of boarding, lessons and training was just not enough and the "milk check" had been eaten away to nothing.

So we did it! Just like the rock climber when he sees what looks like a good ledge to grasp, but it is really far away and may even be beyond reach. But maybe, just maybe, if they give it one good push of energy and, using all their might, reach and stretch….just maybe it will work. So, on October of 2006 we made our last large credit-card purchase and I signed up for a workshop to become certified in equine-assisted learning.

Chapter 8
Hope

The summer of 2006 was emotionally and physically draining. In our weakened state of being we had not put hay in the hayloft at the horse barn, for the first time in our twenty-year marriage. The representatives from government agencies were still on the farm, and by this time it was too hard to get out of bed, let alone sling 400 bales of seventy pounds each into the hot, sticky hayloft. We had hay bales stored in other barns throughout the farm, and that is what I was doing on that memorable spring day in 2007.

Robert and I had made it through many conversations of throwing our hands up, selling it all, getting a divorce, and going our separate ways. Instead, the conversations had turned to morning meetings of sharing the books we were reading. Gradually, they started to turn into spiritual conversations of all denominations and perspectives. However, the past six years had been filled with anger, bitterness, regrets and sadness that stuck to us like flies on a fly-strip hanging in a barn. And it was a slow and gradual process to rid ourselves of the residual negative effects of the experience.

By this time, I had been using the ***breathing*** exercises on a regular basis. I would practice them in the barn before, during and after training sessions with various horses. I started to observe and note the different equine behaviors that resulted from the various ways I would ***breathe. Slow, even breaths would yield a calm, relaxed horse***, while short, rapid breaths would yield a scared, fearful horse ready to fight.

At times, I would take my yoga practice out to the pasture. Just as on the day with Cheyenne, I would place a blanket under what we now call "The Tree of Life" which is near the spot I described earlier. It was as though the herd of horses were leading me down the path of learning how to ***quiet my mind, gradually and ultimately relaxing my body*** in return. It was as if the horses were guiding me on a journey to free me from the cage of my own ***thoughts and emotions*** that was trapping me within the painful emotional existence that had become my new reality. The entire herd, in one way or another, was leading me to greener pastures, similar to the way in which a lead mare would lead the herd to water or greener pastures. If they weren't leading, they were validating my journey, offering support and encouragement through their actions and reactions. Whether it was joining me during a yoga stretch, or a muzzle on the head, it was as though they were giving me the feedback of a truth they innately knew and that I was going through the ebb and flow to find.

It was a nice spring morning and I fired up the old van to load up hay for the horses. Robert had left hours before to complete the morning milking of the cows. I thought I was in a good place; Robert had recently told me I was grinding my teeth less at night; and generally, things were starting to look up. Even though the equine-assisted learning workshop was a good experience, it was not exactly what I was searching for. Nonetheless, I had some individuals boarding their horses in the barn who were willing to participants as volunteers as I practiced my newfound adventure. Thus, things were looking up; we had a plan and we were making some strides toward getting out of this mess.

We were working hard to implement the *positive thinking, visualizations and gratitude* concepts we were reading about and watching on the host of library books and DVDs. As I walked to the mailbox, I would replace the vision of bills spilling out with a *visualization* of checks coming in from the equine-facilitated learning business I was attempting to create. In an attempt to "re-train" our brains, we had decided that it was a blessing that the September 2002 meeting had taken place before we acted on our plans to build a new equine facility. Just two weeks prior to that meeting, I had paid an architect to draw up plans. I had put the plans on a shelf to support Robert and his dreams, just as so many women over the years have done before me. And although I experienced frustration and sadness, I felt at the time that it was the correct thing to do. After all, the equine business was a supplemental income and not our primary income, so I had to get the priorities straight. The look of a traditional barn is different from that of one to host equine-facilitated learning services in the way I wished. So, we would openly *express the gratitude* we felt that this had occurred and we would attempt to find the positive in every experience that our new belief-system was working to create.

With our new financial reality, building a new equine facility was out of the question so we began to develop a new plan. We had planned on re-purposing the lumber from the old dairy barn that the government agencies were requesting us to tear down. It was a huge rustic barn that looked, to non-creative thinkers, like a heap of rubble. But to us, it was the boost we needed, the supplies we could use, and the hope we were searching for, until.....

As I steered the old van around the last curve before the dairy barn, it hit me like a brick wall. Cranes, bulldozers, dump trucks, strange and not-so-strange men were walking around everywhere. My throat seized up, I started gasping for breath, but nothing would go past my closed-up throat. What? Why? Weren't they supposed to give us notice? No! No! No....This couldn't be happening!

It was as if the hopes of a brighter tomorrow, the hopes of all my dreams, heck, the hopes of just surviving this nightmare, were jerked out from under me like a rug. All the positive thinking in the world drained out of me in that unforgettable moment. I had never before, nor ever since, experienced the depths of the darkest emotions that took hold of my body and paralyzed it as it did that day.

I opened the door to the van and stepped out to walk over to the men and ask them what was going on. Unfortunately, my body had other plans. It was not cooperating with my head. My knees buckled, refusing to listen to my head asking them to walk. I fell to the ground. Twice I attempted to get up, but with the same results. The thoughts of the barn left my head, to be replaced with fear and confusion over what my body was doing. I was trying to call out for help, but nothing was working, my body was paralyzed, and my voice was silenced. Robert was milking in the new facility that was situated at the top of a hill. "How am I going to get there?" I thought to myself.

The answer came quite unexpectedly. Robert came when he heard a man yelling at me. He screamed, "Get up! Get up and get out of our way! We have spent way too much time here and you are holding us up!" My head was trying to scream, "I am trying!" But nothing but tears came. By the time Robert made it down to me it had felt as though someone was pulling at my chest, yanking on my shirt. My head is swirling; this can't be happening, it just can't be.

It was Robert's turn to coach me through the breathing, *"Breathe in and out,* honey." "What are we going to do?" I asked. "That was the last plan I had, honey, we need the timbers from the old barn to build onto the barn and possibly a place to live" I told Robert through the tears. Slowly, with the *breathing in and out,* my body and *thoughts* started to settle. And the problem-solver in me gradually started to come back. "I just can't sit by and do nothing. We have to do something!" I told him.

I thought: "I know! We can call our pastor and ask her to come pray with us. Oh, wait, that could be embarrassing, as we quit going to church years ago." .... "I know—a protest! I can call people and the newspaper to come see what is happening! I can chain myself to something to stop the machinery!" And then the strangest thought came to me. Earlier in the week, our neighbor had been featured in the local newspaper for a *drumming* practice she had started to explore and enjoy. Robert had been reading about Native American cultures and *drumming.* So I called her, and asked her to join us in a *drumming ceremony.* It was our first such experience, and one that we have continued ever since, both with and without the horses.

Much to my surprise, the *drumming* stopped the workers dead in their tracks! And it was the break I needed to give myself a chance to breathe and prepare for the ultimate destruction of the barns. Fortunately, we were able to gather a small supply of old barn siding that would eventually be used to help us bring our new equine-facilitated learning program from the *visualization to reality*.

And to this day, when we run into some of the local workers they still ask us, "Why *drumming*?" "I have no idea, it's just what came to me *in the moment*, much to my own surprise," I would reply.

Chapter 9
Thriving not Surviving

Ring….Ring….The phone call came seven months after the *drumming* ceremony we had at the barn that spring day. It had been a rough year, but we were moving forward. We were practicing *quieting the mind* and searching to find the *positive* in each perceivable negative. We jokingly told each other, "It can't get any worse, so we are moving forward!" That was until I received the call.

"Mrs. Jeffers?" The voice on the other end asked. "This is she," I replied. "I am really sorry to tell you this over the phone, but I feel it is really important to get moving on it right away," she continued. "What?" I asked. "Well, Mrs. Jeffers, your mammogram did not come back good. I am afraid….I am afraid you have cancer, Mrs. Jeffers. I'm sorry, ma'am. You are in Stage 4, and I am making the recommendation for you to be referred to the James

Cancer Center in Columbus. You should be receiving a call soon regarding scheduling of your appointment. Again, I am sorry," she said as she hung up....silence.

I slowly hung up the phone and turned to the children and Robert. "I have...I have cancer," I slowly said. It took a while to shake the shock: "I have cancer." Hmm, now the problem-solver in me again had nothing....nothing.... or did I? It was as if I was standing in the batter's cage, feeling stronger and ready to grab the latch on the door, just to have that darn machine start back up, throwing more and more balls at me! I had worked so hard to get up out of the fetal position, and I was not about to go back there! I have a choice, I have the *power within*, and I would remind myself daily. I can choose to take the cancer journey as a victim, which defines me as a pink ribbon on my lapel or a bumper sticker on my car. Or I can stand up in that dreaded batter's cage and look the cancer in the eye, as I had been working on for the past four years. And once again, some days were easier than others.

Research shows that how you handle stress can have an impact on your physical health, so it really was not a big surprise once I took time to think about it. But now, how were we to navigate the "big C" within our new belief system? When you say "cancer," or "the big C," people usually give you the deer-in-the-headlights look, as thoughts and emotions come to the surface of someone they knew or loved having had the disease. You can feel the fear radiating around the room. I made a vow to myself to attempt to use all the skills and techniques I had been studying, for the past year, to feed the *positive*, not the fear and negativity, throughout this journey.

The cancer journey began with that first appointment. Robert and I were escorted from office to office, down this corridor and that one, this test, that test, see this nurse, now that one. My head was spinning, but I felt my body comply with the requests and I remember wondering whether this was how a cow feels being gently nudged down cattle chutes making a turn here and there, not really knowing what the destination looks like?

The experience of MRIs, X-rays, looking through pictures of reconstruction options, or not, and the explanations of the procedure for marker-placements was all leading ultimately to the mastectomy. And throughout the metaphorical cattle chute, I was able to use my newfound skills to keep the "what ifs?" at bay, *quiet the mind and practice living in the moment.* To this day, however, the most memorable experience, which I treasure with *gratitude*, came during the marker-placement procedure.

I had been told that it was a two-hour procedure. But it seemed as though time stood still—perhaps forty-five minutes, tops. I was able to meditate and use what I found out later was similar to the practice of Centering Prayer. I remember asking God, in whatever form God exists, to be with me, in *silence, and hold me in love.* I was able to find and hold the silence that sparked the most beautiful *light* deep within me; it led to an overwhelming *inner peace*. Not sure what to call the presence—God, Creator, Universe or any other name—I eventually decided it did not matter what I called it. And I remember wondering "Could the intensely beautiful light actually be God? Could the intense energy of unconditional love, in the form of light be God?" As I reflected on the experience I also remembered being in church all those years hearing the Pastor say the words "Peace be with you" and the congregation reply back "And also with you."

For the first time, I felt the peace. The overwhelming *sense of peace, in that moment,* came only when I *quieted my thoughts* and the fearful emotions that tend to follow many of them. Over the years, my *thoughts and the emotions* that proceeded from them had become the batter's cage that had obstructed my view of this magnificent *sense of freedom.* It is strange, but when I allowed myself to feel life instead of think about life, I became freer, and it took *quieting the mind* to find it. Interestingly, I found it through the lens of what is typically one of most fearsome experiences: cancer.

Several weeks later I awoke from my mastectomy surgery. Upon awakening, I remember seeing things with more clarity than ever before. It was as if the new lens allowed me the opportunity to see the world with brighter, more vivid colors, with a crispness I had not seen before.

And in that very moment, in the midst of what should have and would have been my darkest times and deepest fears, I gained a newfound *appreciation* for the gifts that life has to offer us. Each moment has something to offer us in the form of a lesson or new experience, whether it is perceivably good or bad.

Our society has placed so much emphasis on material possessions. Technology can *connect* and disconnect us all in one moment, but in the end our souls yearn for a *true connection*. Not an artificially-driven one, but one deep from the *heart and soul*, like the *connection* I felt through the light during that procedure. Words on this page cannot even begin to describe the *sense of peace through the connection* that I felt that day. So, in the moments following the surgery I started down the journey of discovering a newfound *appreciation* for all the gifts big or small, family and friends, the beautiful colors on a butterfly, the delicate nature of a single dandelion, and all the gifts and lessons the horses had given us.

After the surgery, I was instructed to go home and rest. I was told to schedule a follow-up appointment for two weeks later to begin physical therapy to regain the range of motion on my right side. My chest now sported a seven-and-a-half-inch suture that ran from my armpit to the middle of my chest. A drain tube was laced directly under the skin and was attached to a container that could be clipped to my clothing. They had removed six lymph nodes during the surgery, disrupting the tissue and muscle in the chest wall on that side. I was home for a day or perhaps two, and I felt I needed to go to the horse barn. For my entire life, since I was ten years old, the barn represented safety and solitude in this chaotic world. Whether it was to cry, **breathe** or celebrate, the barn has always been my "go-to." But this time was different.

The first day, I wanted to just get back to a normal existence. So I tucked my drain tube up under my shirt and, in spite of my family's disapproval, I went to the barn. Just as in the past four years, the moment was filled with emotional and physical pain. The difference was that, spiritually, things had changed. I still carried the *peace in my heart and the stillness in my head;* I just wanted to be with the horses. And as always, they were there.

As I sat on the same ledge as I have for many years, I took my *long, deep breaths.* Through some tears of joy for the good news that it was In situ, which means it had not spread, tears of joy for being back home in the barn and tears of sadness for my new body, I stayed there with them just taking *in the moment with pure gratitude* that I am sure comes from looking one's own mortality in the eyes. And as I sat there, the horses once again led me down a path of healing.

I could not move my right arm up more than a few inches, so I chose to grab a brush and brush the smallest horse in the herd, Cameron's pony, Pepper. I brushed to the best of my ability and strength that day. Being a recreation-therapist and having the determination of a bull, I choose to create my own physical therapy, my way. "I absolutely will not be a victim!" I told myself. "I have STOOD UP and I am walking out of this batter's cage one way or the other!" I could hear myself telling myself this over and over.

Each day I would go to the barn multiple times, and groom a horse. I gradually worked my way up to taller and taller horses: Pepper, Cheyenne, and finally William. William is a 16.3-hand horse, and reaching him was a major challenge—and my ultimate triumph. I would end each grooming-session by slowly inching my right arm up to reach the withers—the high bone on the base of the horse's mane and neck—and I placed my left hand on its chest. I would image a *beautiful rainbow from my heart to theirs*. I would *thank* them for all their *unconditional love* and the guidance they had given our family through the years. All the while, I would receive their *unconditional love* no matter what my "new-to-me body" looked like. It was a beautiful exchange of *gratitude and love* that gave me the strength and courage to open that metaphorical batter's cage and walk out! I was in control! No more wishes, fears, and thoughts of "What if? What should I or should I not do, what should I or should I not say, think or feel!" I am back!

For the previous year, I had been kicking along the new equine-facilitated learning program I chose to call Natural Freedom. Again, I had to push away the fears and uncertainty when someone would ask "Shouldn't ranch or farm be in the name?" "NO! The program I wish to share with others is a direct result and a creation of the journey out of that batter's cage; it is a feeling, not a place. I did not just go to a weekend workshop and open the doors to provide services. I lived this amazing journey to share it with others, a journey that started by *looking within*, and ended with a *freedom* to call my own; yes….the name is Natural Freedom.

In the beginning, it was a very new concept in our area, and I had been sending letters out, making phone calls, inquiring and knocking on doors for presentations, and offering demonstrations. I got a big opportunity to meet with a community member to discuss the program, and I was not going to miss it! I remember the day very well. I got dressed, tucked that drain tube up under my shirt as I had been doing for a week or so when I went to the barn. I hoped and prayed that it would not fall out during the meeting, and it didn't!

Soon afterward, I went to my follow-up appointment to remove the tube and start physical therapy. "What have you been doing?" the physical therapist asked. "Oh, no—what? Is something wrong?" I asked. "No, not at all!" she replied. "Whatever you are doing, just keep it up. You do not need me at all—your range of motion on your right side is the best I have ever seen at this stage after a mastectomy." OK then, back to the barn I go!

Chapter 10
Drumming

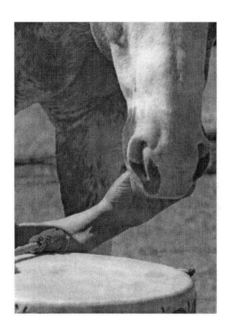

As the numbness of hearing the words "You have cancer" gradually receded, and the overwhelming sense of *connection* that I experienced during the cancer surgery engulfed me, life seemed so *much calmer,* filled with *hope*

and a newfound *appreciation* for life's journey. This sent me searching for more spiritual *connections*, workshops and experiences. Robert and I were both holding down multiple jobs to dig ourselves out of our financial hole, and money was still not freely-flowing to accommodate anything lavish. I did hope, though, to find something close to home and cost-efficient. Luckily, I happened to find a spiritual workshop being offered several miles up the road, and it offered the option of working off the fee! "Perfect," I thought to myself. I sent out an email stating our circumstances, and *thankfully* our application was chosen.

Robert attended the majority of workshop sessions, while I fulfilled the work duties. Interestingly enough, there was a drum-making session included among the weekend events. It had not been listed in the details, but Robert was excited to hear about the opportunity. He made one drum at the event, and brought the supplies home to complete mine at a later time.

After the weekend was over, he continued to play his drum after work every evening. He was like a child playing with a new toy. At night, after the daily chores, he would bring the drum out and play while I finished up the horse-barn duties. One of the first evenings of *drumming*, the horses had a very interesting reaction to the drum, which I eventually wrote about on a listserve I had joined to *connect* with other equine-facilitated learning pioneers and providers. On May 7, 2009 I wrote the following on PATH EFMHA Open Yahoo group:

Good Morning!

I am one of the ones that are lurking in the background on this post, learning and becoming inspired by this wise group. However, I feel compelled to share some thoughts and a personal story regarding drumming and the herd of horses we have been blessed to care for.

My husband had attended a spiritual and renewal retreat for his own personal growth. This retreat offered an element of making your own drum. Upon his return from the retreat, he had come out to the barn to share. We often mix our interests, as his first love is not the horses as it is for me. Anyway, he was sitting in the aisle intently drumming.

On our farm, I try to offer the horses as many choices as possible, one of them being the choice to come into a stall in the morning or evening depending on the time of year, and the choice to leave and go back out into the 70 acre field. On this day, as every other day, I closed the front barn doors and opened the back door that leads to the field. My husband continued to drum and was obviously in his own world, enjoying his new drum. I was dumbfounded as to what happened next. The horses literally created a line in the aisle way, each horse, in turn, stopping by my husband for approx. 30 sec. each, then moved on, but not out into the field. They entered a stall until there was space to re-enter the line, circling through for several rotations before proceeding to the field.

As you can imagine, this led to some very interesting conversations between the two of us. Conversation about why they had this reaction. At first we thought it was the rhythm, however after other drumming times with them we have since come to the conclusion that it is not this, but rather the inner state of being of the person that is drumming. We have played around with various different scenarios with our own family, not clients. We have been out in the field with the herd and passed the drum around with each of our family members given a chance to explore. Depending on the person drumming, different horses have left the herd to join us in our family "drumming circle."

The last time we played around with the drum and the horses my husband had had a rough day. He was sitting in the same place as usual, but you could tell he was forcing the drumming, not flowing as usual. The horses were unusually restless. The horse I was grooming started to become fidgety in the cross ties, the one boarded horse in the barn was cribbing, one was pawing on the stall doors and another was circling. I remember thinking they are trying to tell me they are ready to go out and I started finishing up with the horse I was grooming. All of a sudden, there was a shift in the barn and all the horses activity stopped. The heads went low, soft eyes, utter silence... I looked over and paid more attention to the drumming and it sounded different. My husband noted later that he had a hard time getting into the drumming, that he was forcing it and drumming from his head, not his heart in the beginning, but finally got there later.

Our conclusion: It does not matter what rhythm, whether it is soft or loud, fast or slow, etc. The horses reactions have shown us, once again, our inner state of being at any given moment. This has led us to have a better understanding on the effects of the various states of consciousness on ourselves, others and our surroundings.

Has anyone else had similar experiences?

Peace,

Pam Jeffers

Two years later, after securing a contract with a local behavioral health center, I attended several workshops with social workers I was working with to provide equine-facilitated learning and therapy services. One of the workshops was titled The Impact of Trauma and Neglect on the Developing Child, run by Dr. Bruce Perry. He was sharing his research results and subsequent model of treatment for children who experience traumatic events such as abuse or family violence. His workshop reviewed the effects of mistreatment on the brain of a child and his recommended treatment based on this research.

He and other trauma experts have identified that the human brain organizes itself from the bottom up, meaning that a person needs to feel safe and relaxed in order to tap into other parts of the brain such as problem-solving and **relationship interactions**. According to them, when humans go into the fight-or-flight state of being, all the other parts of the brain shut down, leaving them in an alarmed state of being. According to Dr. Perry's research, this primitive, survival part of our brain needs to calm down before we can tap into other parts of our brain. He went on to state that he advocates the use of "rhythmic repetitive" activities to aid in this process.

That's it! I finally had the answer to the question "Why *drumming*?" And why the "Turban Lady!" It all made so much sense now. Without even knowing it, our bodies were finding the "rhythmic repetitive" activities that made sense to us during the journey out of the metaphorical batter's cage. We drummed, groomed horses, practiced yoga, and engaged in centered breathing exercises, while our son took up skateboarding. All of these were examples like those that Dr. Perry gave for helping to calm the alarmed state of being the brain goes into when a threat is perceived.

Our family had been living in a constant state of alarm for some time. "Where are we going to live if the farm gets foreclosed on? How are we going to pay this bill, that bill? How are we going to get LaTicia the medical care she needs? How do we get Robert's blood pressure down? How are the kids going to go to college?" All these questions and so many more were swirling in our heads on a daily basis, and no wonder! Without knowing it, we started seeking, exploring and ultimately finding ways to calm our "scared brain" so that we could use our higher level of thinking and feeling the *connections* of everything around us.

Maybe the *drumming* experience in the barn with the horses lining up was providing us with a visual to understand this concept. Perhaps the horses became *calm* when Robert found the *inner peace* away from the mind-chatter of his working day. Perhaps the horses enjoyed their scared brains' relaxing into a *calmer existence with the rhythm of the drum* that night and wanted to move into the *space of peace* just as much as we did.

Many people flock to the beaches for vacations every year—could this be what we are doing? Listening to the ocean flow up on the beach has a soothing rhythmic, repetitive sound. Listening to the soft breeze blow through the leaves, or watching the flight patterns of birds, can have a similar effect. But what if we were to use this information and the resources we have directly in front of us every day to aid in keeping our "scared brain" as calm as possible? Would our relationships with others improve? Would we as a society be able to act through the lens of love rather than that of fear?

At the time our team attended the Dr. Bruce Perry workshop, the services at Natural Freedom already consisted of elements our family had used to get out of the batter's cage. Activities such as *the centered breathing* exercises, *guided breathing* exercises with the horse, grooming to *calm and connect*, not to clean, mindful activities of listening to the horses munching on the hay, were all part of the program. We had implemented many of these years earlier, but now we had science to back up the "why." And this allowed us to expand further to include other opportunities that the natural world has to offer us, as humans, to *calm* our brains. In doing so, the stage is set to tap into the emotional brain and improve the *relationships* around us, be it with self, horse or others.

We now had scientific proof of why we were interested in incorporating another tool our family had learned during the chaos of the preceding years. And I had one more reason to *be thankful* for the experience.

Chapter 11
Seeing Within

I could not name a single person who told us that we could be successful in starting Natural Freedom. "How are you going to do a program in that old barn?" "You don't even have an indoor to work with." "You don't know anything about business, you will not be successful." "You don't even have a tractor." "You should offer your program at my place where it is more pristine." "I could do that." These are a few of the negative comments I received in the beginning. With the exception of our not understanding business, most were true statements. The fact was that our facility was an old, renovated dairy facility built in 1930s by Robert's great-grandfather, and the odds of success were definitely stacked against us. We had an old facility, no access to start-up money, bills stacked up high, and at the time no one in our service region understood or had even heard of equine-facilitated learning.

The true essence of a person, however, is not in what you see, but what is within. And I had the determination, the passion, the personal journey and the years of experience with horses that many did not see, whether by choice or otherwise; top that off with a supportive, talented, hard-working husband and two children who knew—though they may not have liked it at the time— the importance of huddling around a family goal. My family was like the herd of horses coming together in the common goal of moving together for the greater good, working together, making sacrifices; together we were able to debunk all the negative perceptions of who we were and what we had to offer. I had a big dream and the willingness to put the energy and intent into creating it. And so the work began.

The naysayers did have a point. Even though the barn had had horses in it for years, it was in need of many improvements before we could bring clientele in and out on a regular basis. The barn entrance had a low spot directly in front of it that created a massive mud puddle when it rained. There were no walkways, nor any shaded area for our *centered breathing*, which I wanted to incorporate into the program. Again, our thinking brain needed to kick into overdrive and find creative solutions with the limited resources we had at hand. Interestingly, in the end, many of these creative solutions provided additional benefits to our program later as our services grew and the program expanded.

We began by moving rocks from the farm and strategically placing them in patio fashion in front of the barn. We felt this would serve two purposes. First, it gave a more aesthetically-pleasing look to the entrance. Second, we were able to eliminate the lower surface that led to the mud puddles. As the program grew, however, we began using the rocks as markers for children to stand on and to engage in a modified version of *centered breathing* exercises. It is now a staple of our services to find a rock, "put glue on your feet," and take three *long, deep breaths* before entering the barn. This serves two purposes: first, it aids in helping calm our brains down. Second, it provides a model approach for respectfully entering the horses' personal space.

Our first demonstration of many was in the fall of 2007. We used a painted door on saw-horses for refreshments, literature tables, and straw bales for seating. Luckily, the county had hired tree-trimmers to clear the branches on our road. I flagged them down and asked if they could dump their chips beside the barn. We used these as a path to the outdoor seating area.

We were able to salvage a small pile of siding from the old dairy barn that had been demolished on that memorable spring day. Robert moved the pile up to our horse barn, now the home of Natural Freedom, and built an addition onto the existing barn to provide us with a shaded area. And I hand-painted a sign on the old barn siding, hung it proudly and moved from hoping to knowing the *vision* would come to fruition in due time. We just had to *believe* and continuing *working towards it*.

Chapter 12
The Big Break

Throughout the journey of escaping the batter's cage of chaos, there was no pivotal moment when I could say there was a magic wand, or Cinderella slipper, that was the defining moment of shifting our lives from a mad, sad, fearful existence to joy and *love* for life again. As much as I wished for it to happen early in the journey, the feeling of moving from a perceivable hell to experiencing heaven on Earth was a long, seemingly-endless one filled with baby steps of accomplishments and setbacks along the way. Winning the lottery was out of the question, as you have to play to win, and there was absolutely no way we could spend any money to buy tickets. Admittedly, there were days when I secretly wished that a miracle would happen and that we would experience some miraculous fairytale ending. But the reality is that **happiness comes from**

the heart, with our thoughts and perceptions leading the way. So, even if there was not a miraculously huge extrinsic gift to change our reality, there were enough little ones to give us a bread-crumb path of *hope* and a *true appreciation for the power within.* Extrinsic, material rewards can be fun in the moment, but will eventually fade over time. Intrinsic rewards, however, can be a life-changing experience—though not without daily work on awareness of *thoughts, emotions, energy and effort,* at least for us.

And the creation of Natural Freedom took on the same painstakingly slow process to become a reality. The year of 2007 began the continuous, diligent pursuit of partnerships with agencies, professionals, funders and private personal-development clients. I called and knocked on any and all doors for the opportunity to speak, give presentations and/or meet with anyone interested in this new approach to learning and healing. The agencies and organizations I ended up speaking with were diverse in nature.

I did not have a preconceived idea of a population to serve, as I truly believe that at the core of our being we are all humans with a unique story of personal triumphs and hurdles. My educational background in therapeutic recreation gave me a foundation that enabled me to meet any population or individual where they were, and to adapt activities, as appropriate, to meet those needs and interests. And I was eager to provide equine-facilitated services in some capacity. So I spoke at cancer initiatives, local university schools, professionals serving the geriatric population, local county children services representatives, private practice counselors and a local behavioral-health agency, to name a few.

I was able to pick up a few private-pay personal-development clients, and grant-funded programs such as the Rural Medicine Program, where I helped a medical student to gain knowledge about improving doctor-patient relationship skills and about unique rural needs, using a curriculum by Dr. Beverly Kane called *The Manual of Medicine and Horsemanship: Transforming the Doctor-Patient Relationship with Equine-Assisted Learning.*

Our big opportunity, though, came on March 12, 2009, when I was invited to present at a local community mental health agency. I had been meeting with an old acquaintance who was interested in writing grants for Natural Freedom. She had taken a temporary position at the agency on the child team and had graciously inquired about their interest in hearing about this unique opportunity.

Nervously, I packed up the literature I had managed to compile by using my paychecks from the part-time position I had managed to pick up a year and a half earlier. This was a holiday position of unloading trucks at 5:00 a.m., which gradually turned into a sales position and eventually that of manager of the home department. The small paychecks went to make our credit-card payments; anything left over was used to set up Natural Freedom. So with nerves on high alert, and *pride and hope in my heart*, I stepped into a room full of mental-health providers serving the youth in our area, and made my pitch.

Yes! All the hard work had paid off! One of the social workers who specialized in serving post-adoption families was interested in partnering to serve her families! She was also one of the leading local specialists in developmental trauma. She was very knowledgeable and motivated to find innovative ways to make a difference in the lives of the clients she served. The agency gave us one shot at proving the effectiveness of the program. They agreed to a partnership to provide services for one pilot-family for one year, with some stipulations including that of no horseback riding being allowed.

We set out to develop just that—an entirely-new program for our area. We spent endless hours working together. While I shared my knowledge of equine behaviors and the techniques our family had used to move out of chaos, my partner shared her knowledge of the social-work field and especially of treatment for individuals who have undergone traumatic experiences. It was fascinating how easily the two worlds came together. She would inform me of the treatment goals, and I would modify a traditional groundwork activity that I had used for years.

Over the years, I have attended many horse clinics, watched DVDs and read books by all the great trainers:

Ray Hunt, John Lyons, Mark Rashid, Chris Irwin and Pat Parelli, to name a few. Though I am not one to follow one particular program, I was always able to take at least one piece from their words of wisdom, and to bring it home to use with the horses I was working with. I used the same process here, blended the knowledge I had accumulated over the years with horses, listened intently to the knowledge of the mental-health provider, and attended multiple workshops and trainings. Eventually, we teamed up with an extremely-knowledgeable psychologist and a leading expert in attachment and bonding for developmental trauma. Together, we went on to provide trainings in our area to share the program we had developed.

True to the entire journey, however, the one-year pilot program represented a wonderful opportunity signifying one baby-step in accomplishment, but creation of Natural Freedom's services did not come without setbacks. Throughout the journey, we endured the local politics of funders and professionals, mergers that influenced the growth of the program, and additional equine-facilitated learning programs coming into our region, to name a few of the stumbling-blocks along the way. Each hurdle, however, gave me a new opportunity for practicing my newfound *self-awareness*. I had the power to withstand each and every one—or did I? Life kept asking the question; for me the trick was to STAND UP to the test of time!

Chapter 13
Cup of Tea?

In 2008, the year of cancer and the summer before beginning the pilot program, I was still providing traditional horseback-riding lessons as well as working at the local department store. The hand-painted Natural Freedom sign had been hanging on the old barn for approximately a year. And even though I had a few clients, I was still knocking on doors and attempting to share the word of equine-facilitated learning in our region.

I was giving a traditional riding lesson when a maroon Cadillac pulled into the driveway to look at the Natural Freedom sign. My heart started racing, and I could feel the enthusiasm bubble up inside of me. I had been practicing the positive thinking my Dad preached about when I was growing up. I had completed a vision-board two years earlier, and practiced "seeing" it on a daily basis. So I just knew, with all the cells in my body, that the person who pulled up into the driveway was interested in our equine-facilitated personal development services—I just knew it!

I asked the intermediate rider to continue practicing an exercise we had been working on, as I attempted to walk over casually to the car and introduce myself. My hands were shaking so hard that my fingers had a difficult time manipulating the chain latch on the gate. "Come on fingers, you have done this millions of times, please cooperate!" I told myself. I managed to make my way over to the middle-aged woman and said, "Good afternoon, ma'am, my name is Pam. How may I help you?"

In the next moment, my confidence popped like a cartoon bubble and poof....it was gone. "Is the address of this place 41810 State Farm Road?" She asked. "Hmm, well that is a strange question," I remember thinking. "Yes, it is, can I help you with anything?" I asked her. She looked down at her lap as she softly stated, "I am with the bank that holds the mortgage to this property, and I am here to take pictures as it goes into foreclosure." "Oh....oh, OK," I could hear myself saying. I remember thinking, "Here it is. I have a choice—what's it going to be, Pam?"

In that moment, I could have returned to the anger and frustration of feeling vulnerable and at the mercy of a larger entity. And that would have been a much-easier path to take, a path of casting out the anger at feeling the injustice of being a part of "the Barn Project" and the subsequent housing bubble. I could have succumbed to all the judgements and misperceptions cast onto us based on assumptions about our challenging financial situation. During this time, we had been answering endless phone calls, just to hear on the other end, "Are you planning on keeping your home?" "YES, we are going to keep our home and NO, I am not going back into that batter's cage; I am where I am but that does not define me!" I thought. It surprised both of us when I replied, "I understand you have a job to do; how can I help make it easier? Feel free to walk around and take all the pictures you need. If you wait a minute, I can finish up in the arena and give you a tour. Would you like to come inside and take pictures? Would you like a cup of tea? I know you have a job to do, and so do I. I would love to sit, drink tea and explain our services, because, yes, we plan on keeping our place." The calm, confidence and determination in my voice and body were all welcome.

Unfortunately, I would have more opportunities to continue using the skills I had developed to tap into my *calm brain,* as other events and situations arose along the journey. But each one provided me the opportunity to practice making a *calm, positive* response when faced with adversity. Admittedly, sometimes it was easier said than done, and sometimes I felt more triumphant than other times.

Chapter 14

Heart to Heart Rainbow

Our one-year pilot program began in August 2009, and with it began an intensive educational experience for me in trauma and attachment. Eventually, our team grew to include four of us: I, as the equine specialist; the local social-worker trauma expert; a local psychologist in private practice; and an attachment specialist from central Ohio. Among the three of them I was immersed in a vast amount of knowledge about trauma.

What I learned from them in those four years was amazing, and deeply-*appreciated*! I learned about the research of the leading experts in the field of trauma and attachment, such as Dr. Bessel van der Kolk, Dr. Daniel J. Siegel, Dr. Bruce Perry, and the Heart Math Institute. I learned about the biological responses of the autonomic nervous system, and the adverse effects trauma has on the system. I learned about the neurobiology findings and attachment research, mirror neurons, and the science of the heart. Between the knowledge of these three professionals and the research in their profession they graciously shared with me, I was inundated with valuable knowledge to digest, absorb and ponder.

I attempted to digest each new workshop, training or body of knowledge they shared, and over our time together it led to much reflection on my and my family's healing journey. Each piece of new information led to contemplation. I spent endless hours pondering the correlations of the research findings, not only with our journey, but with horse-human relationships in general. The scientific research provided so much valuable information that could be applied in treatment or personal-growth opportunities in the equine-facilitated learning field. Additionally, I felt that it could be applied for the purpose of improving horse-human relationships on a personal level.

Many of these research findings are complex, and difficult to understand in detail. What I was able to comprehend, however, and to apply as an equine specialist practicing in the field of equine-facilitated learning, aligned with many of my personal beliefs and experiences. And the events our family had experienced with our horses during the journey of finding the ability to STAND UP in the batter's cage strongly aligned with the research findings I learned about during those beginning years of Natural Freedom.

The leading experts discuss the importance of *calming the self* when it comes to the treatment of trauma. The human body consists of the autonomic nervous system, which includes both the sympathetic nervous system and the parasympathetic nervous system. The sympathetic nervous system is the part of human physiology that was designed to protect us from life-threatening danger. When this system kicks into gear whether due to a real or to a perceived danger, it pumps blood and heightens the senses designed to take care of us in a threatening situation. The heart rate increases, breathing gets shallow, and muscles tense as the body prepares to take care of the "danger." The fight-or-flight response kicks in.

Conversely, the parasympathetic nervous system helps the system rest, calm down and recover. People who have undergone traumatic experiences tend to default to the fight-flight system (sympathetic) more quickly because of their experiences. Practicing skills that aid the ability to tap into the calm and recovering system (parasympathetic) can be helpful. The leading experts advocate beginning trauma treatment with activities that provide individuals with opportunities to *calm the brain*. This can be done in numerous ways.

"So this must have been why learning the breathing techniques were so helpful," I thought to myself. This is also why I was adamant about starting each session with a *breathing* exercise with our pilot family, and with the many families that followed.

I found out later that it was the description of the *breathing* exercises that initially captured the social worker's attention on the first meeting. I had described this during that March meeting for the child team of providers. Little did I know that what I was presenting to them was what they had learned at their trauma trainings? It was meant to be.

It was approximately two years after my cancer journey when one of the team members told me about the Heart Math tool. She had shared it with many of the families she served. The Heart Math Institute has led the way in gaining knowledge of the full capacity of the heart, beyond its basic task of pumping blood throughout the body.

Their studies show that a person's thoughts, and subsequent emotions triggered by the thoughts, affect the heart in a negative or positive manner, depending on whether the emotions are rooted in a positive or a negative feeling. The positive emotion has been found to provide a more-orderly and harmonious synchronized-heart-rate variability (HRV), meaning there is a more consistent rhythm between heartbeats. These studies have also suggested that the electromagnetic field the heart creates can affect the brain, so that the heart and brain have a continuous pathway that influences the functioning of each. Additionally, the electromagnetic field has been discovered to have an impact on other individuals around them (see www.heartmath.org).

"Was this what my gut or my heart was seeking when I went out the barn those early days after my mastectomy surgery?" I asked myself. I had managed to perfect the deep *breathing* and meditation, Centering Prayer calming practice of tapping into my parasympathetic system when I enjoyed the "light" during the cancer procedures. But the Heart-to-Heart Rainbow practice came later, as I searched for a way to show the horses my *gratitude* for their unconditional love and for the guidance they had provided along the path of our healing. Was the Heart-to-Heart Rainbow my intuitive way of finding what Heart Math calls their "heart-based positive emotion-focused techniques" to aid in finding a more harmonious HRV?

Our team incorporated the Heart-to-Heart Rainbow into the service for the post-adoption family for that first-year pilot program in 2010. By the end of that year, the results of the program were favorable, and the community behavioral health agency renewed our contract to serve more post-adoption families. Our team continued to use the *centered breathing* exercise and the Heart-to-Heart Rainbow, to facilitate relationship development.

Children who have experienced trauma tend to have difficulty connecting with others. Thus, by using the scientific research and personal experiences with the horses, our team created the program that was later included in one of the first books published as a resource for licensed professional counselors in incorporating Equine-Assisted Counseling into their practices. Written by me, Erin Lucas and Kristina Houser, the article "Heart-to-Heart Rainbow: An Imagery Experience to Facilitate Relationship Development" appeared in the book Harnessing the Power of Equine Assisted Counseling: Adding Animal Assisted Therapy to Your Practice, edited by Kay Sudekum Trotter, and published in 2012.

Our family went on an emotionally-chaotic journey, and the eventual relief from the situation came through *connections with self, horse and others*. Now Natural Freedom's unique model of practice began to form before our eyes, as our team provided more and more services. Exploring inner-relationship- and self-awareness skills by spending respectful time in activities with the horse, and offering mindful, non-judgmental guidance in transferring skills for improving relationships with others, became the cornerstone of our program.

Chapter 15

STAND UP

Once again, the big break did not come without setbacks. It was early in the year of 2010, perhaps in January or February that the notice came via certified mail. I am unsure of the date, because it is the only event that I consciously made the choice not to put on the calendars that I kept along the journey. I am not sure why I chose to keep the calendars unless it was my way of attempting to organize the disorganized brain that I had endured throughout our experiences. The certified letter, though, was something I wanted to keep from my children, so I did not put it down in writing.

On that cold winter day, the mail came with the usual share of bills. Over the past years, these had gradually slowed down, as I attempted to take responsibility to the best of our ability. I had contacted all our creditors either to pay them off or to make payment arrangements. The sale of our rental properties had been used to make payments, but had not completely paid off the balances on most of the cards. So we had set up payment agreements. But what I did not know was that all the payments I was making for the past three years with the paychecks from my part-time department-store employment were not even covering the interest on the credit cards—let alone all the principal balances and the fees that had been added to the accounts. So when the time-stamped, prearranged monthly payments expired, full payment was demanded immediately, which of course we did not have.

I recall the phone calls very well. "Mrs. Jeffers, you owe $_____; may I process that check today?" they would ask me. "I do wish I could, sir," I would reply. "Are you disputing the charges, ma'am?" he or she would continue. "No, I am not," I would reply. "You made these charges; you owe them, ma'am," they continued. "Yes, sir, I did, and I will pay if it takes until I am eighty years old, but I cannot pay today, I am sorry," I replied. The next comments varied over time and according to whether I was able to use my skills to calm myself down and tap into my parasympathetic system or whether the "fight" of my sympathetic system kicked in.

I admit that in the beginning I would yell. It did not feel good to be in this position, and it was very foreign to me. The natural instinct of my ego to defend my worth would take over in the blink of an eye! After the cancer journey, however, I became able to remain calm even in the midst of the perceived judgements cast upon me throughout the endless phone calls.

In one day, one of the major banks had called fourteen times, repeating the same degrading message of how irresponsible I was—as if I were making up my excuses and holding out on them, just choosing not to pay for our purchases as well as all the fees and interest that had now accrued to an astronomical amount. It was fascinating to witness the reactions I received, depending on my ability to do my inner work and tap into my calm brain rather than respond in fear and humiliation to what I perceived as attempts to degrade and antagonize me into feeling unworthy.

All choices have consequences, whether these that elicit happy and joyful emotions or sad and fearful ones; either way, the consequences are the inevitable result of our own choices. I had made the choice to use the credit cards with the hope and dream that we would increase our income-base more quickly than we had, while the banks had made the choice to increase the interest rate and to impose astronomical extra fees and charges. So here we both were, looking at the consequences of our actions, and it gave me a chance to STAND UP, quite literally, and look that batter's cage in the eye one last time.

As I was getting dressed, with the mantra "They cannot eat me, I can do this," repeatedly running through my head, I looked out our bedroom window that has a gorgeous view of the rolling hills of southeast Ohio. As I was taking my slow, easy breaths in hopes of staying in my calm brain, a beautiful, large red-tail hawk came swooping down and landed in a small tree that stood not fifteen feet from the back of the house.

According to what we had read, some Native Americans believe that animals come into our lives to provide life-lessons, and their animal spirit-guide messages had sparked in Robert and me many interesting conversations and topics to ponder. According to this Native American belief system, the red-tail hawk is a sign from the higher source and can offer strength in difficult times. For me, watching the birds soar in the sky had given me much-needed opportunities to stay in the moment and practice improving the coherency of my heart-rate along the healing journey. This beautiful bird was a welcome sight to me as I approached the potentially-scary experience I was about to undergo.

Robert gently reached over to hold my hand as we made our way up the long flight of outdoor steps up to the second-floor main entrance of the courthouse. We were like fish out of water as we entered the main doors and showed an employee our certified court order to appear today. She gave us the directions we needed.

We made our way up the next flight of steps and stepped into the hallway where many others were sitting on the benches waiting to go into the courtroom. Apparently, the looks on our faces, and our non-verbal cues, were as obvious as the awkwardness we both felt inside. "Ma'am, you're not familiar with the procedure, are you?" a gentleman kindly asked in a soft voice. "No sir, I'm not," I could hear myself reply. "Don't worry, I'll help you," he said.

"The people call Pam Jeffers." The words came from the open door. "Follow me," the gentleman said. Robert and I slowly made our way through the crowded hallway and followed the kind gentleman into the courtroom. "Sir, you need to sit here." He gestured to Robert. "Ma'am, follow me to the front," he said. I remember thinking, "What? Robert can't come with me? I am all alone....breathe, Pam, they can't eat you." The gentleman pointed to the chair and gestured to me to sit down and he softly whispered in my ear with great kindness, "Ma'am, just do what I tell you and you'll be just fine." I could feel myself nod in agreement, but no words came out of my mouth.

There was a gentle tap on my shoulder and a finger pointing for me to STAND UP as I heard the words "All rise!" The judge came into the courtroom and stated clearly, "_____Bank vs. Pam Jeffers is now in session. You may sit." I casually glanced over to the kind gentleman standing beside me, as he nodded and softly mouthed the words, "Go ahead, sit down now; it will be OK." And he turned and walked to the back of the courtroom. As he left me all alone, my attention was brought back to the front of the courtroom, where I could hear the judge say, "Are you Pam Jeffers?" "Yes, sir," I could hear my shaky voice reply.

"_____Bank?"….Silence. "_____Bank?" Silence….

The judged had a perplexed look on his face as he shuffled the papers. I could hear his deep sighing breaths of frustration as he read the papers, looked up at me and finally asked the kind gentleman to get him a phone. While we waited for his return, the judge made casual conversation with Robert and me, explaining that this was a rather-unusual circumstance.

Apparently, it is unusual in credit-card cases for the defendant to show up. The judge continued to mumble under his breath, "Well, I guess they were not planning on you showing up, and now I have a situation." He called the bank several times, and with each attempt his frustration appeared to mount. "Well, ma'am, I sure wish I could throw this out of court, but the way it is written they will just be coming back. But I am not happy with the lack of presence. Thank you for coming. New paperwork will be written up and a new court date will be set," he stated. The kind gentleman casually walked back up from the back of the room to escort me out, and with a smile I expressed my ***deepest gratitude*** for his kindness and assistance. I had STOOD UP and looked that pitching machine square in the eye. No, they did not eat me, and I lived to tell about it, but now what?

Just as with the kind gentleman in the courthouse, life has an interesting way of putting people and situations into your path that can assist you in navigating life's journey. The kind gentleman made a huge positive impact on that day's journey, one I will always remember. He was able to take a very scary situation and make it bearable. We are all able to have an impact on others, if we wish. It could be as simple as holding the door open, with a smile, for a mother struggling to navigate a stroller through the doorway; it could be helping an elderly person reach groceries from the top shelf. Simply put, a small gesture might be all someone needs to get through a challenging day or circumstances.

Several days later, life gave us another gift. Robert happened to run into an old friend, the fellow soccer-mom who had called to inform us of the accidental death of Cameron's best friend. She is an attorney with a practice in the Columbus area, and had been traveling back and forth to work from our small hometown. She had recently decided to move her practice to our town and purchased a building that needed repairs. She knew that Robert worked in construction, and flagged him down to inquire about hiring someone, asking for recommendations. Robert quickly replied, "I would gladly help you out. How about a trade? "Sounds good to me," she replied, after hearing of our pending lawsuit with the bank. Within two years, we had made an agreement with the bank and paid off our debt, and she had a beautiful new office.

Big accomplishments, small steps and minor setbacks had become my normal way of living. But with hopes of a brighter tomorrow, believing in a dream and hard work,

I was able to remember to hold my head high, keep my eye on the vision of a goal, and not allow the actions or words of others to keep me from STANDING UP to my full potential!

Chapter 16
Free Yourself to be Yourself

"It is upon disaster that good fortune rests." This year marks fifteen years since that memorable fall meeting in 2002, and eleven years of providing equine-facilitated learning services as Natural Freedom. Though it was a painful journey to get here, I can now read the quotation from the Taoist sage with full understanding and appreciation. Without the "disaster" in our family's lives, our life would not have the look it has today. This "disaster" led me, us, down an amazing personal journey of strength and courage that probably would not have happened without the negative experiences that made me want to "Stop and Start Over," as the famous Ray Hunt saying goes.

Natural Freedom, just like our family's journey, was filled with many hurdles, with big accomplishments and stumbling blocks along the way. However, like our family, Natural Freedom has proven to stand the test of time, struggles and triumphs paving the path of "freeing ourselves to be ourselves."

Both of our children have graduated from college and are bringing their gifts to the world. The path they had to take along the way was far from what I had envisioned as I held them in my arms as babies. As I had to remind myself daily during the journey out of the batter's cage, however, they would ultimately receive far more from the experience that they would have if things had worked out to be like the fairy-tale vision in my head. They learned that their story does not have to define their future. They learned how to hold their heads high, embrace their story, and reach their highest potential because of it, not in spite of it! They learned that with a clear vision and goal, hard work and dedication, and belief in themselves, they could do anything they put their minds to. Looking within, you can see with clarity and purity, and by *quieting the mind and connecting with the heart,* you can do anything you put your mind to.

Our Family: (left to right): Cameron, LaTicia,
Pam and Robert

Initially, we envisioned an equine-facilitated learning program as a supplement to our family income, along with the traditional horsemanship program that I was already running. But the journey soon turned into much more. The experiences of our family were far too rich to keep to ourselves, so the vision of Natural Freedom was born. We wanted to share the gifts of the horses and of nature with others. Never could I have imagined that eleven years later the center would be supporting Robert and me along with two other full-time team members. With seasonal fluctuations, our team of four qualified specialists in mental health and learning and the equine field serves an average of 65-110 people per week. We provide services in behavioral health, wellness workshops and retreats, personal development, family services and educational opportunities to name a few. We have met many beautiful individuals, families and professionals along this journey. Yes, indeed, "In disaster good fortune can rest," but we must be ready, willing and able to see it.

Our society is running at such a fast pace, with many advances in technology and the same old yearnings for the trappings of success. Whether in the hustle and bustle of rush hour, walking down the street, or in the grocery store, one can see the effects of disconnection. Many times one can see the "should have, have to, could have" mindset on the faces of those around us. I admit that I can easily fall back into those patterns, without consciously working on my inner self. With the help of the "disaster," however,

I am much more aware of such thoughts when they sneak up on me and I have the tools to address them.

Even though support from family, friends and horses in my life was invaluable and deeply appreciated, ultimately no one could help me out of the batter's cage but myself. As I explored and strengthened my *self-awareness and gained a deeper relationship* with my own thoughts, emotions and actions, the horses, as always, walked beside me on the journey. And as always, they provided that non-judgmental feedback of wanting to spend more time walking beside me when I was able to *quiet the mind and open the heart.*

This personal journey, coupled with the scientific research behind it, provides a natural baseline of information to help explore improving relationships, whether the intent is for the *relationship with self, with horses, or with other people.* Beginning from the concepts of *quieting the mind, opening the heart,* and walking alongside the spirit of the horse, we at Natural Freedom have been able to create the *"C" Within Model of Practice.* It is rooted in rich research, personal stories, and many hours of experience serving others at the Natural Freedom Wellness Center. Whether the focus is on *Relationship with self, with horse, or with others, the "C" Within Model of Practice* offers five principles for exploring and expanding relationships.

Natural Freedom Team: (left to right)
Robert, Pam, Janessa and LaTicia

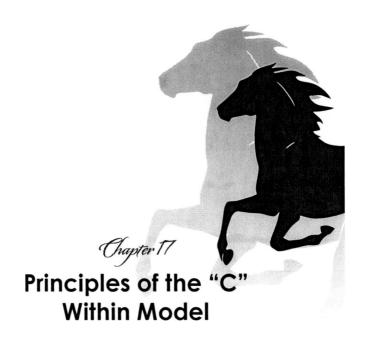

Chapter 17

Principles of the "C"
Within Model

Centering and Grounding the Self

Our model of practice begins with activities and exercises that provide the opportunity to quiet the mind. Early in the journey, Cheyenne led us down the path to begin the practice of slowing our thoughts and living in the moment, and it has grown from there. We have found that the horses appear to be more likely to want to spend time with humans when we attempt to calm the "sympathetic" system down and practice being present in our thoughts. With practice, this skill becomes easier to tap into when the "scared or anxious" brain kicks in, whether due to performance anxiety in the horse-show arena, or the social anxiety of being with others. A herd of horses will exhibit heightened anxiety, with head up and nostrils flaring, when they perceive a threat in their environment. Once that threat is gone and the situation is seen as safe, the horses will "return to grazing," quickly reverting to a calm state.

Unfortunately, humans tend to hold onto the effects of the "scared brain" longer than do horses, and often need to consciously "reset" themselves, using self-regulation skills to create a space between completing one task and beginning another. Scientific research indicates that this skill is good for humans, and horses appear to prefer it when humans can quiet their minds and regulate their emotions. We can reset ourselves, become more in touch with where our thoughts and emotions are, rather than run from one thought to the next. This sets the stage for proceeding more easily to the next step—connecting through the heart.

Connection through the Heart

As mentioned above, the Heart Math Institute leads research into the science of heart-intelligence. This research is fascinating, and it sheds light onto many questions I have had over the years I have been working with horses. One thing I have observed is that some horse owners, trainers and others have varying reactions and responses to the same horse—sometimes in a positive manner, and sometimes negatively. Ellen Kaye Gehrke, PhD, completed a study of the horse-human heart connection, using the Heart Rate Variability tool (NARHA's Strides magazine, Spring 2010). Her study found that "the rhythm of the person's heart rate variability was more important than whether they had a relationship with the horse," and "The horse's stress level was entirely dependent on the stress level of the human." This is invaluable information not only for the purpose of improving horse/human relationships for personal enjoyment, but also for meeting therapeutic goals within an equine-facilitated learning session. Dr. Gehrke's research also found that "calmness or autonomic state of the horses has a greater influence on the human response than the other way around." Thus, the horse's reaction in a human's presence can be a source of information in exploring within ourselves where our thoughts, emotions and subsequent heart-rate variability are at a given moment, for the purpose of striving for the most respectful relationships, improving self-confidence, improving the relationship with one's own horse, or improving relationships with others.

More research is needed to develop a full understanding of the complexity of the horse-human heart connection. I cannot help but wonder whether many of the great trainers are able to tap more readily into their "calm brain" and to regulate their heart-rhythm in a more synchronized manner than others. Many of us have studied, read and intently watched their methods, with the hope and dream of being able to reach the level of expertise they exhibit with horses. What if we have the ability, and carry the secret to the mystery, the golden slipper or key to success within ourselves, each and every one of us? Perhaps we just need to look within ourselves to see it!

Compassionate Leadership of Self

Early in my horse years, it was common to hear coaches and instructors say, "You have to show them who is boss." And I have watched my share of trainers bring their energy up so high that the horse appears to be fearful of the handler, and to comply with the request out of fear. It just never felt right. Over the years, I have searched for a respectful relationship with the horses, as a partner, and not a domineering one. Throughout our journey and the creation of Natural Freedom, I have done the same. As I was compiling the "C" Within Model, at first I conceived of Compassionate Leadership of the horse. But this still makes the human an authoritarian in the relationship. It occurred to me later that the principle I was really looking for was Compassionate Leadership of Self.

The distinction is important, as it emphasizes the fact that we need to be leading ourselves first of all throughout any relationship. As noted above, science has shown that thoughts and emotions affect our heart-rate variability, which can then be sensed by those around us. Ultimately, holding onto the thoughts and emotions of the "could have, what if, and should have" while interacting with others will ultimately affect the quality of the interaction unless we use self-regulation skills, "reset," and give our full attention to the interaction. Horses are even more tuned into the heart-rate variability, and they give us valuable opportunities to bear witness to what our body is holding onto and carrying into all our relationships. Spending time with the horse allows us to gain awareness of how to take responsibility of our thoughts, intentions and energy, in ways that can improve our relationship skills.

On May 12, 2007, Robert and I scrimped and saved and were able to gather up enough to attend a Ray Hunt clinic being held in our county. This was the opportunity of a lifetime for me, and even though we could not afford to ride in it, we had saved enough to audit and to buy a small book. I asked Hunt to autograph his Ray Hunt Cowboy Logic book of quotations. His weathered hand reached up to hand the book back to me. That hand held a wisdom that comes only from years of experience. As I slowly reached out to receive the book, he looked up at me and firmly said what he had written in the book: "Think."

As our healing journey and Natural Freedom continued to unfold, and the science came to light, his instructions resonated with deeper meaning, and with more intensity. Being aware of your thoughts and of the emotions that go along with them makes us understand what the horses and others around us feel from our heart-rate variability and electromagnetic field. What if a truly remarkable horse/human relationship begins with the human taking full responsibility for himself; his thoughts, his emotions, with the intention of living from the heart, moment to moment, like a beautiful dance of energy, moving together in a manner respectful to both entities?

Several years ago, I watched a Mark Rashid clinic where he stated that the horse/human relationship is 50/50, as all relationships are. 50% of the responsibility for the relationship is on the human side, while the other 50% is on the horse. All choices ultimately have consequences, but as the humans it is our responsibility to establish expectations within the relationship. Whether it is a horse/human or human/human relationship, we can set the expectations that we feel are respectful but, ultimately, horse or human has the freedom to choose to engage respectfully in the relationship, accepting the expectations, challenging them, or moving away from the relationship because of them. Relationships begin within the self, and respectful activities and exercises with horses can provide valuable opportunities of developing an understanding of the 50% of the relationship we, as humans, are bringing to the relationship as a whole.

Clear Communication

Most of the workshops and clinics I have attended over the years have discussed the communication elements of horse/human relationships. Chris Irwin's Horses Don't Lie was a groundbreaking book on how horses can teach us about ourselves. He was one of the pioneers to dive into the concepts of congruency, and how our inside needs to match the outside to connect effectively with the horse.

Many other successful trainers have shared their knowledge of communication with the horse: body-awareness, focus, intention, energy, and clear visions are all elements I have studied thanks to many of these great trainers. The bottom line, however, is that communicating clearly is how we relate with the horse. What is our body saying, and do our thoughts and emotions match what our body is asking the horse to do—in other words, does the inside match the outside, as Chris Irwin mentioned all those years ago? Now the science of the human world provides another piece of the puzzle of exploring how and why this concept is important when it comes to relationships. From the inside and out, horses' sense and respond to the 50% of the relationship we bring into the arena. Whether it is in the arena with horse/human relationships for the purpose of improving human/human relationships, or a horse/human relationship for personal experiences, it is our responsibility to do the work within the "arena of life" out of respect for all. Spending time with the horse using the scientific research available and taking responsibility to explore ourselves from the inside out can help us gain newfound appreciation for improved relationships overall.

Cognizant Appreciation

Masaru Emoto was a Japanese researcher who studied the molecular structure of water. According to his research, human consciousness has an effect on water molecules. His findings were that water molecules respond differently to positive thoughts and words directed at them than to hateful, angry ones. In the YouTube video "Water, Consciousness & Intent: Dr. Masaru Emoto," the water molecules that experienced the words "love" and "thank you" are beautiful and majestic snowflakes in appearance, while mean and hateful words change the molecules into a dark, pitted formation.

Thought, words and deeds have a powerful influence, positively or negatively. Research in many venues is showing that it really does not take much to make a positive difference on another being, and this holds true in horse/ human relationships and subsequent human/human relationships. Though it may be kind to buy and/or do something to show appreciation, is it the only way to show appreciation? Our human brains often feel compelled to give, buy or do something to show our appreciation, when perhaps the most powerful thing we can actually do is say nice words or find pure, unconditional love in our hearts. It may feel good to buy your horse the fancy new pink bell boots, fancy halter or purple saddle-pad but, beyond the physical necessities for existence, perhaps the biggest gift we can give them or each other is a quiet mind, an open heart, and improved awareness of our inner self. Where are our thoughts, emotions, intentions, and energy, and do they all align for the greater good of improving relationships? Asking these questions could be the beginning to "C"ing more clearly.

"C" Within is about seeing through a new lens—come join us.

Bibliography

Bryne, Rhonda & Harrington, Paul. *The Secret.* Dharma Production, 2006.

Chopra, Deepak & Tanzi, Rudolph E. *Super Brain: Unleashing the Explosive Power of your Mind to*

Maximize Health, Happiness and Spiritual Well-Being. Potter/Ten Speed/Harmony, 2012.

Chopra, Deepak. *The Seven Spiritual Laws of Success.* Novato, CA: New World Library, 1994.

Chopra, Deepak & Tracy, Kristine. *On My Way to a Happy Life.* Carlsbad, CA: Hay House USA, 2010.

Gee, Judee. *Intuition: Awakening Your Inner Guide.* New York: NY: Barnes & Noble, Inc., 1999.

Gilbert, Elizabeth. *Eat, Pray, Love.* New York, NY: Penguin Random House, 2006.

Hempfling, Klaus Ferdinand. *The Horse Seeks Me: The Path to an Understanding of Equine Body Language.* London: Cadmos Publishing Ltd., 2010.

Hoffman, Matthew. *What the Bleep Do We Know?* William Arntz and Betsy Chasse Producers, 2004.

Hunt, Ray. *Cowboy Logic:* Bruce Publishing Ltd., 2004.

Irwin, Chris. *Dancing with Your Dark Horse: How Horse Sense Helps Us Find Balance, Strength and Wisdom.* New York, NY: Marlowe & Company, 2005.

Irwin, Chris. *Horses Don't Lie: What horse teach us about our natural capacity for awareness, confidence, courage and trust.* Cambridge, MA: Da Capo Press, 1998, 2001.

Jeffers, Pam. *What Cheyenne Knew, Angels on Earth.* New York, NY: Guidepost Publication. May/June 2010.

Kane, Beverly. *The Manual of Medicine and Horsemanship: Transforming the Doctor-Patient Relationship with Equine-Assisted Learning.* Bloomington, IN: AuthorHouse, 2007.

Kaur, Gurutej. *Kundalini Yoga for Balanced Chakras: Stimulate the body's energy centers.* Spirit Voyage Records, 2006.

Keating, Thomas. *Intimacy With God: An Introduction to Centering Prayer.* New York, NY: The Crossroad Publishing Company, 1994, 200

Kohanov, Linda. *Riding Between the World's: Expanding Your Potential Through the Way of the Horse.* Navato, CA: New World Library, 2003.

Kohanov, Linda. *The Tao of Equus: A Woman's Journey of Healing & Transformation through the Way of the Horse.* Novato, CA: New World Library, 2001.

Kohanov, Linda. *Way of the Horse: Equine Archetypes for Self-Discovery.* Novato, CA: New World Library, 2007.

McCormick, Adele von Rust & McCormick, Deborah. *Heart Sense and the Human Heart.* Deerfield Beach, FL: Health Communications, Inc. 1997.

Parelli, Pat & Kadash, K. *Natural-Horse-Man-Ship.* Colorado Springs, CO: Western Horseman Magazine, 1993.

Peale, Norman Vincent. *How to Be Your Best: A Treasury of Practical Ideas.* Pawling, NY: Foundation for Christian Living, 1990.

Perry, Bruce. *Building Better Lives: Changing the Cycle of Child Abuse and Family Violence. Overview of the Neurosequential Model of Therapeutics.* Columbus, OH, Workshop by

Franklin County Family and First Council, April 25, 2012.

Rashid, Mark. *Horsemanship Through Life*, Boulder, CO: Johnson Brooks/Big Earth Publishing, 2005.

Rashid, Mark. *Whole Heart, Whole Horse: Building Trust Between Horse and Rider*. New York, NY: Skyhorse Publishing, 2009.

Siegel, Dan J. & Hartzell, Mary. *Parenting from the Inside Out: How a Deeper Understanding Can Help You Raise Children Who Thrive*. New York, NY: Jeremy P. Tarcher/Penguin/Penguin Group (USA) Inc., 2003.

Strozzi, Ariana. *Horse Sense for the Leader Within: Are You Leading Your Life or is it Leading You?* Bloomington, IN: AuthorHouse, 2004.

Swift, Sally. *Centered Riding*. North Pomfret, Vermont: St. Martin's Press, 1985.

Tolle, Eckart. *A New Earth: Awakening to Your Life's Purpose*. New York, NY: Penguin USA, 2008.

Trotter, Kay Sudekum. *Harnessing the Power of Equine Assisted Counseling: Adding Animal Assisted Therapy to Your Practice*. New York, NY: Routledge Taylor & Francis Group 2012.

Walsch, Neale Donald. *Conversations with God: an uncommon dialogue.* New York, NY: G.P. Putnam's Sons, 1995.

Warner, Priscilla. *Learning to Breath: My Yearlong Quest to Bring Calm to My Life.* New York, NY: Free Press/ Simon& Schuster Inc., 2011.

Zukav, Gary. *The Seat of the Soul.* New York, NY: Free Press, 1989.

CPSIA information can be obtained
at www.ICGtesting.com
Printed in the USA
FFOW04n0841290317
33994FF